To Paul, forever and ever, amen!

From Ordinary to Extraordinary

From Ordinary to Extraordinary

Breaking the Chains of Ordinary to Walk in Your God-Given Purpose

CANDY RAINES

Section 1
Introduction

For most of my life, I felt hopelessly ordinary. You know, just an average person trying to make a go at something greater and often coming up short. I think many of us struggle with feelings of inadequacy and long desperately for something more in our lives. This book delves into the notion of how the same feelings I suffered from can stop many of us from pursuing the amazing calling God has for our lives.

There have been many books published in the last twenty years that speak to the calling or purpose that we all have, but none really look at the biggest roadblock that keeps us from our destiny: our doubts about ourselves, our calling, and our abilities. Perhaps, like me, you feel too ordinary for God to use you for any great purpose. I invite you, dear friend, to take this journey with me as we explore just what God has planned for our lives and how we can walk with purpose to follow the desires of our hearts.

In the first section of this book, we will search the Word of God to explore just who we are and what God created us to be. The second section explores these feelings of "ordinary," where they come from, and how they stop us from living out our calling. The last section looks at a Kingdom response to feelings of ordinary.

My greatest hope is that somewhere in these pages, you will come to realize that God created you, with all of your struggles and strengths, for a unique and wonder-filled life full of purpose and meaning.

One

Who Am I and Why Am I Here?

*W*hen I was a child, I used to dream about becoming a pilot. I fondly remember riding in the back of my dad's pickup truck (back before the law that prohibits this today) and pretending that I was piloting a jet. I would sit up high on the wheel well, stretch my hands out against the oncoming wind, and imagine turning flips in the air. I loved the feeling of the wind in my face and how it tugged at my long hair.

Unfortunately, by the time I graduated high school, being a pilot had long left my dreams. Reality set in, and I chose to pursue a career in which I could work in the small town where I grew up and simply make a living. Now, when I look back on that dream, I'm not sure why I never thought to follow my heart. Perhaps because it would have been difficult. Or maybe because I thought I didn't have what it took to become a pilot.

We all want to be remembered. To be thought special in some way. We secretly yearn to have that certain something that makes us stand out in a crowd. We want to be a part of something great, to be needed, and to be desired. We long to have skills, abilities, talents, intelligence, and purpose. But the horrible truth is that most of us just don't think we actually possess that elusive quality we have yearned for all of our lives. Most of the time, we walk around feeling anything but special, needed, or vital. What is it that we want? What do our hearts long for with every beat? Why do most of us feel so unfulfilled? Why do we often feel so hopelessly ordinary?

Perhaps you are someone who has never had these kinds of thoughts, and for that, I would call you blessed. Most of us, however, have these thoughts swirling through our heads for most of our lives. Sure, we might discover tiny moments of fulfillment here and there, but the majority of the time, we simply feel unsatisfied with our lives. You might think that these feelings are felt only by unbelievers, but the harsh reality is that even most Christians struggle with these emotions of inadequacy and unfulfillment throughout their lives. Most of us God followers have heard the expression about how we all have "a God-sized hole in our hearts" and how only God can fill that hole. For certain, this is a true statement. Our Creator made us to have a relationship with him, and when we do not have that relationship, we feel empty. So why do those of us who are connected to our Creator still yearn for something more? Isn't he enough? He should be, right?

I was introduced to God at a young age, and I asked him to come into my heart when I was around the age of five. I have had a relationship with him for most of my life. Sure, I have had some ups and downs (that will be another book!), but I have always tried to please God with my life and to live for him. I have been involved in church activities, leading worship and teaching, for most of my life. But still, there has always been this deep, gut-wrenching desire to have more, to be more. More what? I didn't really know at first. I just always assumed that perhaps I was lacking in my faith and, for some reason, doubt had crept into my mind. So, like many, I stuffed those feelings down deep. I hid them where no one else could see them.

A relationship with God through Christ is certainly what our Creator desires, but he created us for more than to simply know him. He created us with specific purposes in mind. To understand this, we must first understand that the process of creation is exactly that: a process. It is not a one-time event, over and done in a day. God is continually creating us. Yes, there was a beginning, but there will be no end.

The Creator's voice is magical. It is alive. It is active and always moving. When he speaks, the vibrations don't wax and wane and eventually die away as they do in the physical world. The echoes from his spoken Word go on for eternity. When he spoke us into existence, our souls were destined to endure for all time. Now add to this the fact that God has a very specific purpose in mind for each soul he created.

When he thought of us (before we were formed in our mothers' wombs), he had grand things in mind. He spoke our names, and we were formed. His spoken word caused a miracle to happen when the cells from your parents combined to form the beginnings of your human body and God's breath was breathed into that body in the form of your soul. His spoken Word is never meant to be still—it travels through space and time. And he continues to speak new thoughts and plans to our souls every moment of every day. We were thus created in his image to be in motion: dynamic and never ending. We are continually being created to fulfill a very specific role in our world, a role that no one else on earth could ever fill.

When we live our lives as though we are static creatures, here today and gone tomorrow, we are leaving out something vital in our nature: the vibrant role God intended for us. This is why we often feel unfulfilled even when we accept Christ as our savior, because we know the Creator but fail to understand or walk according to the role or purpose for which we were created.

Perhaps we do this on purpose, seeking to rebel against our heavenly Father. Maybe we want to live our own lives without his interference. If that is you, I pray that you will come to know your true Father and his will for your life. But I am mostly speaking to those who know their Father—the King of Kings, the Creator of the universe, the beginning and end of all things—and yet still feel as though they are not enough.

There are many good books out there that speak about finding one's purpose, and they are certainly excellent in helping us to seek God's will for our lives. I have read many of those books and found them to be very compelling. So when God asked me to write this book, I wondered why he would take me down a path that so many have traveled before. I feel as though he wanted me to back up a bit and explore the reasons *why* I felt so underqualified to do his work, to understand why feeling "ordinary" has kept me from walking in his will for so many years. I needed him to reveal these deep doubts and fears inside me and my human response to those fears in order to fully grasp his calling for my life. Just to know that I had a God-purpose was not enough. I needed more.

For many years, I have felt the desire to write a Christian book. For most of my life, on nights when I couldn't sleep, I would make up stories in my mind to pass the time. When I began to put these thougths on paper, I attempted to write a novel and only finished half of it. I just couldn't complete it. Then I wrote a nonfiction Christian book and was almost finished, but, for some reason, I couldn't bring myself to get it published. This went on for years. I put aside those desires many times in favor of busyness. I was busy raising kids. I was busy getting my degree. I was busy at work. I was busy being a good wife. The list was endless. But mainly, I just felt that I did not have the skill or the knowledge to complete the task. This past summer, while recovering from back surgery, I was complaining to my mother-in-law about how bored I was because I couldn't do anything of a physical nature and needed something to fill the time while I was recuperating. "You know," she said, "you have always wanted to write a book. Why don't you use the time to do that?"

I hadn't had any good ideas in a while, so I mulled it over in my mind for several days. Then one night as I was praying, I brought up the subject again with my Father. I told him that if I were to write a book, he would have to give me the subject because I had absolutely no ideas for a new book and didn't feel that I was supposed to revisit the ones I had started in the past. I told him that it would have to be all him! I needed anointing not only on my abilities but on the whole book: the subject, the content, the Scriptures, all of it. That night, as I lay down to sleep, I wondered why I had always had the desire to write a book but didn't have what it took to get it done. I just felt like I was too ordinary of a person to actually do it. As I began to pray and think about my doubts, my Father began flooding my mind. My Creator was speaking to me and through me. He had something to say to me, and in doing so, he was also inspiring me to take that message to others.

My thoughts began to revolve around why he had given me the desire to write books even though I never felt that I was gifted enough to do so. In my mind, I was just this normal, middle-class, working woman who was not good enough to experience success in something as important as writing anything of value that would help other people grow closer to God. I also had a desire to be a speaker and to share the insights that I felt God was giving me, but I could come up with even more excuses for why I was not doing that. Excuses started popping into my head like, *I'm not talented enough, I don't have the skills I would need, I don't have the drive, I don't speak well, I am not good-looking enough, I don't have the right personality, I'm not smart enough,* and even, *Maybe that's not really my calling,* started popping into my head. Finally, to sum up all of my shortcomings, I told God that I was just too ordinary to do any of those things. I think he actually laughed at me! He said, "I have prepared a feast for you. You cannot even begin to imagine what I have in store for you. I created you, and I knew what I was doing. Do you trust me?"

I was absolutely floored! He was saying he wanted me to pursue my dreams, and in doing so, he was going to teach me what he has been trying to teach all of us through his Word for so long. He showed me that many others like me let feelings of being ordinary stop us from walking in the calling he has for our lives. He wants us to understand what his Word says about his will for us, why we doubt what he has called us to do, how we respond to feelings of being "ordinary," and how we can have a Kingdom response to his calling instead.

The next day, I sat down to write, and the ideas just began to inundate my mind. As long as I kept writing, the thoughts kept coming. It was like a computer download: The information just kept coming and coming.

So, in the following pages, we are going to explore what his Word, the Bible, says about all of this, and we are going to do it together—you and me. I must tell you I am not a pastor. I am not an evangelist. I am not an internationally known speaker. I am not a theologian. I am just an ordinary woman doing extraordinary things through God's anointing and his will for my life. We are going to go through this journey together. Are you ready to start living the life you were created to live?

Two

What God's Word Says About Me

*I*f someone were to ask "who are you?" how would you
answer? Would you tell them about your job or what you

do for a living? Would you tell them about your role as a father, mother, son, daughter, wife, husband, uncle, or grandparent? How about your hobbies; would you mention that you are an avid golfer or that you love to hike? Would you describe your personality? Would you say you are an introvert, an extrovert, type A, easygoing, or that you have a sarcastic side to you?

Psychologists tell us that one of the basic human needs is significance—to *matter*. Abraham Maslow's famous hierarchy of needs theory listed the need to be loved and to belong right below physical and safety needs. We need to be a part of something. In other words, we need to have a purpose. This is because we were created with a purpose in mind. We were created not only to have a relationship with God but to walk with him daily. Consider Adam and Eve in the Garden of Eden. They walked with God every evening. From the beginning, we were designed to live out our lives in relationship with our Creator.

For I know the plans I have for you," says the Lord. "They are plans for good and not for disaster, to give you a future and a hope.

—JEREMIAH 29:11 (NEW LIVING TRANSLATION)

To know that God plans things for our good is a comforting promise from the Father to his children. It certainly brings peace when we are struggling and going through trials.

When I began praying about how feeling ordinary stops us from fulfilling God's purpose for our lives, I began looking at God's Word through a new lens. In the past, I had interpreted this verse to mean that God was going to work all things for *my* good and for *my* future, no matter what I did or where I went. But a second look tells us that he knows the plans that *he* has for us. The Father has written *his* plan on our hearts, and *his* plan is for good and not for disaster. *His* plan is to give us a future and a hope.

Too often we go through life making random decisions, and then, when things don't work out, we plead for God to fix our messes. How often do we stop and pray about God's will for our lives before we make decisions? Sometimes this can be very frightening. We may feel the Father tug on our hearts to do something out of our character, so we push his voice aside in favor of our own will and comfort. We choose what we think is expected of us. We fall back on the routine, the mundane, and the safe. We do this so often that his voice grows dim amid the chaos of our busy lives. I urge you, dear friend, not to let the fear of not being good enough stop you from following God's perfect will for your life.

I want us to look at another verse of scripture into which the Father gave me new insight. Psalm 37:4 of the New Living Translation says, "Take delight in the Lord, and he will give you your heart's desires."

Again, when I read this passage in the past (with human eyes), I always thought he was speaking about giving me anything I wanted. I don't think that this verse is speaking about our needs or wants at all. Of course, our Father loves us and longs to bless us, but in this case, he is not referring to what we want. The psalmist, David, was referring to the fact that God placed his desires in our hearts when he created us. He placed certain desires deep within us—desires that sometimes confuse us or leave us feeling inadequate because we don't know what to do with them. It's almost as if he did this intentionally; we need him in order to determine our purpose.

If we read the surrounding verses in Psalm 37, we see that David is speaking about trusting in the Lord and waiting patiently on him.

> **Trust in the Lord and do good. Then you will live safely in the land and prosper… Commit everything you do to the Lord. Trust him, and he will help you… Be still in the presence of the Lord and wait patiently for him to act… The Lord directs the steps of the godly. He delights in every detail of their lives.**
>
> **—Psalm 37:3–23 (NLT)**

Pursuing the desires that God has given us requires trust! But what greater trust is there than to trust him with the plans and purpose he has for our lives?

Merriam-Webster's online dictionary defines *desire* as "a wish for something or to do something." It also mentions a longing, a formal request or petition for some action, and satisfaction in its attainment. The original Hebrew word for the "desires" in Psalm 37 was *mishalot*, which comes from the word *sha'al*, meaning to "ask or request something" and is based on one's "deepest needs, desires, and questions of our hearts" (hebrew4chritsians.com). Isn't it interesting that when God fashioned us, he placed within us innate questions that lead us to seek him and our purpose in him?

If God tucked certain desires gently into the deep recesses of our hearts, and if we are to take delight in those desires, does this not tell us that he wants us to follow those desires—to pursue them? And if his plan and will for our lives is intermingled with those desires, are we not pursuing his will for our lives when we seek to live out those desires? How awesome it is that once I began to read God's Word without my selfish human aspirations in the way, God began to open up more and more of his promises! Those promises speak volumes about his perfect will. God's Word is true, and we can take it at face value. But often there are multiple layers of promises within a single passage, so we must dig deeper into his Word.

Now, let me make something clear right away. When God's Word speaks about *desires* in these verses, he is not speaking about our sinful nature, our flesh, or our cravings for sin. The desires he is speaking about are the ones he placed deep in our souls. God's desires never equal sin. Rather, these are the desires that align with his will. The desires I want you to explore in this book are the God-given ones that align with his plan and purpose, not our sinful nature.

So now there is no condemnation for those who belong to Christ Jesus. And because you belong to him, the power of the life-giving Spirit has freed you from the power of sin that leads to death.

—Romans 8:1–2 (NLT)

You might have heard the above scripture while learning about salvation and how Jesus' death and resurrection frees us from the condemnation of our sin. You might be wondering, *How on earth could this scripture speak about anything but salvation?*

The death mentioned in this verse is a spiritual death. God has a plan for you that includes living in relationship with him. Again, this relationship includes walking in communion with him, not just wondering aimlessly through life but being led by his Spirit. Let's look at another verse of scripture tied into the concept of serving God with freedom.

**So whoever knows the right thing to do
and fails to do it, for him it is sin.**

—James 4:17 (NLT)

The phrase "the right thing" is referring to God's commands in the Bible, but it also refers to anything that God asks us to do or not to do. Thus, this is related to his will for our lives. So, because we belong to our Father, his Spirit has freed us from the grip of anything that takes us away from what he desires for our lives.

I wanted to go over this verse first because I personally believed that there were too many roadblocks preventing me from following the desires in my heart. I didn't think I was capable of writing a book. But his Word clearly states that his Spirit has given me power and has freed me from anything that would hinder me from following his will for my life.

Did you catch that? First and foremost, in pursuing God's plan for your life, you need to hear that there is *no condemnation* for the desires he placed in your heart. You are not being selfish if you pursue those dreams. You are not being egotistical. He is not going to chastise you for seeking a change because you feel unhappy about the way your life is going now. His Spirit has broken any chains that would bind you and prevent you from walking in his will. His power is life-giving and will sustain you no matter where you go. Praise God!

Following the scriptures above, Romans 8, verses 14–15 (NLT), tells us:

> **For all who are led by the Spirit of God are children of God. So, you have not received a spirit that makes you fearful slaves. Instead, you received God's Spirit when he adopted you as his own children. Now we call him, "Abba, Father." For his Spirit joins with our spirit to affirm that we are God's children.**

If God has placed a deep desire in your heart and you follow that desire, you are being led by His Spirit, and he calls you his child. He invites us to call him *Abba*, which means "Daddy." We do not need to fear the future, nor to worry about whether we are good enough or smart enough or *whatever* enough to pursue the future we desire. If we are seeking God's plan for our lives, we are accepted. We are adopted into his royal family. He puts his arm around us and calls us "son" or "daughter." His beloved!

Verse 26 of Romans 8 (NLT) says, "And the Holy Spirit helps us in our weakness." Not only did the Father call us for a precise purpose, but his Holy Spirit helps us where we are weak. I don't know about you, but often I feel completely and utterly incapable of doing what I know God has asked me to do. But if we look at the Bible, we find that most of the men and women used by God were imperfect. They had great weaknesses. They needed God to empower them to fulfill the calling he had for their lives. Isn't it wonderful that God knew we would need him? And so he provided for us a Comforter: the Holy Spirit.

I have a friend who is sort of loud. You know, the kind of person who just speaks at a higher volume than most of us. She's animated and outgoing and puts on quite a show at a baseball game! I just love her and her exuberance for life, but sometimes people judge her for this quality. She once shared with me that she had prayed and asked God to help her "tame" her loud and crazy style. God's response was to stop her right in her tracks and ask her why she would want to change the way He created her; he had created her with a loud voice to proclaim his goodness.

There are many times when I do the same thing. I question the Creator by questioning the way he created me. Why do we do this? Why do we doubt that God can take a characteristic that we see as a fault and use it for a unique purpose?

As we continue in Romans 8, we are going to skip down to verses 29–30 (NLT).

For God knew his people in advance, and he chose them to become like his Son, so that his Son would be the firstborn among many brothers and sisters. And having chosen them, he called them to come to him. And having called them, he gave them right standing with himself. And having given them right standing, he gave them his glory.

I have read these verses many times, but in my mission to seek God for guidance in finding and developing my purpose, a new light was shed on his Word here.

I want to simplify what God says about us in these verses to help you see what he does when creating his children. I would ask that you slowly read the following lines aloud to yourself. Stop and think about each one. Notice the order in which he gave the promises.

He knew you.
He chose you.
He called you.
He gave you right standing.
He gave you his glory.

Before he chose you, he knew you. He knew all that you would do: the good, the bad, and the ugly. And still, he chose you. Notice that after he chose you, he called you. After looking forward to all your future failures and still choosing you as his own, he called you for a very specific reason. And after all that, he sent his son, Jesus Christ, to die on a cross to give you right standing with himself (salvation). Lastly, he then gave you his glory (honor). I don't believe that God makes mistakes. He didn't make a mistake in the order in which he listed his promises here, and neither did he make a mistake in creating you for his glorious purpose.

Wow! The first time I fully grasped this concept, I was reading my Bible on my back porch one morning. I literally began to weep. Then I raised my hands to heaven and praised God for His amazing love. My neighbors probably thought I had gone mad!

How awesome it is that our Father knows all of our shortcomings in advance and still has a plan in mind for us? A plan that will bring us acceptance, salvation, and blessings. A plan with a purpose that only he can bring about. A plan that will ultimately bring him glory. This has very little to do with our abilities; it has everything to do with his power and our ability to trust him!

The last verses in this chapter represent the principle verses for this book, and they are verses I would suggest you write down and put in a prominent place where you can see them every day. If you are still reading this book, I assume that like me, you struggle to follow the desires of your heart. Perhaps you also struggle with feelings of being ordinary and letting those feelings stop you from walking the path that God has called you to follow. The following verses are a promise from our Father to people like you and me.

> **And the Father who knows all hearts knows what the Spirit is saying, for the Spirit pleads for us believers in harmony with God's own will. And we know that God causes everything to work together for the good of those who love God and are called according to his purpose for them.**
>
> **—ROMANS 8:27–28 (NLT)**

Your heavenly Father knows your heart because he created you. He knows what his Spirit is trying to draw out of you. He will continue to pursue you and tug on your heartstrings because he loves you and knows that his plan and purpose for you are perfect. He will arrange things and people around you to carry out a work in you because he wants to bless his child. And he wants to use you to bless others.

Our heavenly Father is omnipotent and omniscient. He is all knowing and all-powerful. We humans cannot even begin to imagine who or what he is. We have a very limited understanding of him. One thing I know for sure is that he loves you and me, and he has our good in mind. We may experience great loss or suffering, but I know, beyond a shadow of a doubt, that when we follow the path he has set for us, our lives will be so much more fulfilling. Notice that I don't say our lives will be perfect or easy. We live in a fallen world with sin, sickness, death, and an enemy who longs to destroy us, but our Father God is far greater than all of those things. He will reveal to us, bit by bit, his great love and his plan for our lives.

I hope you are getting the point here. Our Father God has a unique, divine purpose for your life. His will for your life is found in his Word and buried deep down within your heart—a heart that he created to have a great need for him and to fulfill the purpose for which you have been called.

Remember, before he called you, he knew you and still chose you. He did not seek out the perfect person to achieve his plan. No, he had a plan and then created you to satisfy that plan. He knows you are flawed and wants you to continually seek him for help and guidance. Not only does he want us to seek out the purpose for which we were created, but he will give us everything we need to accomplish that purpose.

You need not fear any task he has called you to do, whether great or small. His Spirit joins with your spirit to strengthen and magnify your abilities. His plan is to give you a future and a hope!

Three

WHERE DO FEELINGS OF BEING ORDINARY COME FROM?

*I*t is a great tragedy when someone has a calling or a gift in some area but does not feel as though they can thrive. For some reason, we often recognize the strengths of others but fail to see them in ourselves.

I once met a young man who was so talented at playing guitar that it made my heart ache. He could play any style of music and add so much beauty that one might have assumed he'd had years of experience playing professionally. Unfortunately, he thought he "wasn't good enough" to play with the praise band at church. What could make someone with such a God-given talent think he didn't have what it took to be a part of something so worthy? Why do you and I often let doubts creep into our minds and stop us from pursuing our purpose?

There are three main sources from which these feelings of being ordinary—of not being enough—arise. The first is you. Yes, you read that correctly. *You* are the source of most of our doubts and fears. The second source is other people. The people in your life often play a major role in what you believe about yourself and your calling. And lastly, there can be no doubt that we have an enemy. Satan desires to stop you in your tracks—to prevent you from believing and becoming who God wants you to be.

Your Own Worst Enemy

Henry Ford said, "Whether you believe you can do a thing or not, you are right." Your own beliefs about yourself are fundamental in determining the risks you are willing to take. I have always struggled with low self-esteem and often deceive myself into believing

I am not as good at something as someone else. We all grapple in some way with our self-talk, and what we tell ourselves isn't always correct. The reality can be a far cry from what we believe.

Regardless of our ability to believe in ourselves, there is a deeper spiritual issue that surrounds our doubt about God's purpose for our lives. In the church, I often see people who think less of themselves and attempt to justify it as "humility." But true humility is putting others first, not berating yourself. When we belittle ourselves, we are, in fact, belittling what God created. It is my great belief that we can walk with pride in belonging to God. This type of pride is not a sinful pride by which we position ourselves as superior to others. Instead, we can walk with the assurance that the God of the universe called us by name. We can take great delight in being his.

The Bible speaks about the battle between the flesh and the Spirit. This concept focuses on the fallen nature of humanity and our inability to do what God's Holy Spirit can accomplish in our lives. Thanks to our ongoing struggles with sin, we often think of ourselves as ordinary, normal, commonplace people. Since we struggle with sin, we reason, God must not have a grand of a purpose in mind for us. If he did have some magnificent plan in mind, we wouldn't struggle with falling short of God's commands so often, right? We would be better people. We would be stronger, more pious, more loving, or more determined. Let's see what God's Word says about this:

So I say, let the Holy Spirit guide your lives.
Then you won't be doing what your sinful

> **nature craves. The sinful nature wants to do evil, which is just the opposite of what the Spirit wants. And the Spirit gives us desires that are the opposite of what the sinful nature desires. These two forces are constantly fighting each other, so you are not free to carry out your good intentions.**

> **—GALATIANS 5:16–17 (NLT)**

Again, God brought me to a verse of scripture that I had previously assumed only applied to salvation. This passage sums up the daily struggle in our lives with sin and how we as humans need to surrender daily to God's Holy Spirit in order to let him guide our lives. Once more, there is another layer to his Word that we must peel back in order to understand the full meaning in this passage.

The sinful nature described here is often referred to as "the flesh." Operating in the flesh means doing anything that is in opposition to God's nature. Notice, in the verses above, that the two forces (the flesh and the Spirit) are constantly fighting each other. Picture yourself walking alongside the ocean, trying to remain at the very edge of the water—without ever stepping completely out of it. The waves are incessantly moving back and forth. You can run and chase the waves to try to keep your feet in the water, but you constantly run the risk getting taken under by a huge wave or being left high and dry. It would be impossible to sustain this pursuit for any length of time. It would become a very tiring chore.

We live in a fallen world with the freedom to make our own choices. And yet, our Creator has created us to live in his presence, where peace and wholeness abound. How can we do both? The truth is, we will not be able to accomplish this herculean task until we leave this world and are made into new creatures. Until then, we will continue to struggle between walking in the flesh and walking in his Spirit. Sure, we can become more accomplished at surrendering to his Spirit, but in the end, we still have to keep our feet planted on earth while we reside in these mortal bodies. We will just have to trust the Father and allow his Spirit to guide us as much as possible while on this planet. Throughout our lives, we Christians will constantly have to deal with this battle.

Don't give up on me here. Don't get discouraged. I didn't mention these things to get you down. I want to show you that it is okay when you fail. Failure is a very important part of growing. It's hard. It stinks. Understanding that you are human and yet God still wants to use you is great news!

Notice in Galatians 5:16–17 that we are to let the Holy Spirit guide us. This not only applies to abstaining from sinning, but to whatever his voice is asking us to do. Not only does our sinful nature lure us away from a relationship with God the Father, but it also takes us away from the Father's plan for our lives.

Let's look at the rest of that chapter:

> **Those who belong to Christ Jesus have nailed the passions and desires of their sinful nature to his cross and crucified them there. Since we are living by the Spirit, let us follow the Spirit's leading in every part of our lives.**
>
> **—GALATIANS 5:24–25 (NLT)**

The good news is that Christ overcame our sinful nature on the cross. When we are saved, God no longer looks at us and sees our sinfulness and brokenness; he sees us as pure and whole because our sins are covered by Jesus' blood. Praise God!

When you walk in the Spirit, you can resist the temptation to sin. You can also feel God's purpose and his plan for your life bubbling up inside you. When you walk in the flesh, you sin, and your purpose is held back.

As I started comparing these two paths, God's Word began making it clear what the Spirit inside us is meant to bring. It's almost as if for every argument we could present for why we aren't walking according to our calling, God has an answer.

The Battle between the Flesh and the Spirit

The Flesh	The Spirit
What we see	What God sees: Christ in me (Colossians 3:3)
I am not good enough	God is good, and I am his child (John 1:12)
I can't do it	I can do all things through Christ who gives me strength (Philippians 4:13)
I don't have what it takes	God has not given me a spirit of fear, but of power and love and self-discipline (2 Timothy 1:7)
I am lost	Now I am found (Luke 15)

I am not talented enough	I have spiritual gifts from God (1 Corinthians 12)
I am not smart enough	I have the mind of Christ (1 Corinthians 2:16)
Nothing will ever be enough	God alone is all I need (Psalm 16:5–11)
Believes lies	I know the Truth, and the Truth will set me free (John 8:32)
Dies	Lives forever (John 3:16)
Based on reason and logic	God's wisdom defies logic (Isaiah 55:8)
I don't have any purpose	God has created and called me for a very specific purpose. (Romans 8:28)

What are you going to choose to believe every moment of every day? Are you going to listen to your flesh or are you going to dwell in his Spirit?

As humans, we tend to easily forget God's words. We need to continually surround ourselves with God's Word. I once wrote a list of what God says about me on my bathroom mirror so that I could remind myself multiple times in the day of what my Father says about me. Sometimes I write his words to me on Post-it Notes and stick them on my computer at work. I don't care what you have to do, but you need to learn what God's Spirit says about you and get it into your mind, into your heart, and into your soul. Until you can get past what you are telling yourself about your calling, you will always think you are too ordinary or that you're of no use to God or anyone else. You will never believe what God's Spirit within you can achieve, and you will never know the peace that comes from knowing you are walking a path that your Creator designed just for you.

I have one last thought I would like to share with you on this subject. In 2 Corinthians 12, the Apostle Paul wrote about a "thorn" in his flesh. Many have speculated on the meaning of this statement, proposing that it may have been a physical illness or perhaps the persecution he faced. He did not define what exactly the thorn was.

> **So to keep me from becoming proud, I was given a thorn in my flesh, a messenger from Satan to torment me and keep me from becoming proud. Three different times I begged the Lord to take it away. Each time he said, "My grace is all you need. My power works best in weakness." So now I am glad to boast about my weaknesses, so that the power of Christ can work through me. That's why I take pleasure in my weaknesses, and in the insults, hardships, persecutions, and troubles that I suffer for Christ. For when I am weak, then I am strong.**
>
> **—2 Corinthians 12:7–10 (NLT)**

Perhaps whatever Paul was going through wasn't the actual issue here. Maybe his and our "thorns" aren't really the things which prevent us from pursuing our purpose, but our feelings, perceptions, and anxieties about those things.

Going through tough times and facing obstacles isn't as difficult when you have the right attitude, but many times, emotions tied to those issues can stop you dead in your tracks. Paul talked in the verse above about how a messenger from Satan was sent to torment him and to keep him from becoming proud. Perhaps that messenger was his own mind. The mind is a complex and dynamic organ that often baffles scientists. Psychologists work tirelessly to try to understand the convoluted mess of our thoughts and emotions. Personally, sometimes no matter how hard I try to control my thinking, my emotions just get the best of me. The strongest emotion that hinders us is anxiety. Perhaps this is true for you, too. Anxiety has the potential to change your perspective. Notice, however, that Paul said that his thorn—whatever it was—kept him humble and in a state in which he admitted his weakness and his need for a big God.

I implore you, dear friend—accept that you also might be weak in some areas. Accept that you might sometimes stumble and fall. But, most importantly, accept God's grace. It is a free gift. Receive his power, his forgiveness, his love, and his strength today. They are all you need!

Others

Just as your own attitude and fleshly thoughts can hinder your walk with God, so can the words and actions of others.

Sometimes our self-talk stems from harsh words that were spoken over us at some point in our lives. For instance, when

I was first learning how to play the keyboard, a man in my church decided to share with me just how horrible my playing was. His words were harsh. I tried to banish his words from my mind because I knew he was just kidding, but for many years, I criticized myself for my abilities to play the keyboard. You have probably had similar experiences. Comments like these can be especially damaging when we hear them as children, but regardless, the words and actions of others can affect our beliefs about our God-purpose.

We humans are a selfish lot. We seldom take time out of the day to truly and deeply care for one another. Perhaps this is why Jesus said that one of the greatest commandments was to love one another. We carelessly wander through the day seeking our own selfish desires, often failing to lift up one other with words of encouragement. Sometimes we actually tear each other down in an effort to elevate ourselves. Whether we do this intentionally or unintentionally, the results are the same. We fail to give those around us the love and support they need to live out God's calling in their lives. In other words, if you are waiting for someone around you to tell you your purpose in life or to validate what God has placed in your heart, you might be waiting a long time.

The issue goes much deeper than just needing others to validate who we are. We often have such strong cravings for love and acceptance—from any source—that we go about our lives seeking to please others. Perhaps this is why God's Word warns us over and over again about the dangers of pleasing others. Here are just a few examples from the Scriptures:

Fearing people is a dangerous trap,
but trusting the Lord means safety.

—PROVERBS 29:25 (NLT)

Am I now trying to win the favor and
approval of men, or of God? Or am I
seeking to please someone? If I were still
trying to be popular with men, I would
not be a bond-servant of Christ.

—GALATIANS 1:10 (AMPLIFIED BIBLE)

For we speak as messengers approved
by God to be entrusted with the
Good News. Our purpose is to please
God, not people. He alone examines
the motives of our hearts.

—1 THESSALONIANS 2:4 (NLT)

Then I observed that most people
are motivated to success because they
envy their neighbors. But this, too, is
meaningless—like chasing the wind.

—ECCLESIASTES 4:4 (NLT)

We will never be able to please others completely, nor should we try! As the verse in Ecclesiastes above describes, it is like "chasing the wind." Have *you* ever tried to catch the wind? It is an impossible task. So is pleasing others. We cannot and should not seek to please other people. We should chase after God with all our hearts, minds, and souls.

Here's the deal: No one on earth knows your heart like God. Your Creator knows everything about you. He knew all the days of your life before he even created you. So why would you listen to some human who knows so little about you over the One who formed you in your mother's womb?

Stop letting those around you tell you what you can or can't do. Start telling them what your Father created you to do!

Our Enemy

Have you ever been through a period in your life when you started to question everything you once *knew* was true? Have you ever experienced a flood of doubts about yourself and what God has called you to do?

When people look at me, they often see a person who is very confident in herself and her abilities. What they don't know is that I too am affected by spiritual attacks that feel as though they could crush my soul and bring me to my knees. I can be going along, living my life just fine, when, out of nowhere, I start to experience waves of depression and doubt—doubts about things I never questioned before. We need to recognize these attacks for what they are and from whom they come.

I don't know about you, but I have never actually had a face-to-face encounter with the devil. I couldn't tell you what he looks like, but make no mistake, we have an enemy! If you have accepted Jesus Christ as your Savior and asked him to come into your heart, then you also accepted his mortal enemy: Satan. You have become his target. He knows that he cannot touch God, so he goes after those whom God has called.

There is no greater tool utilized by the enemy than to prevent you from fulfilling your calling—by *convincing you that you are incapable* of doing whatever God has called you to do. Our enemy often stops us from pursuing our calling via the lies we tell ourselves and what others say about us.

Just as God can whisper ideas into your mind, so can the devil. And he can use others to say harsh things about us as well, either to your face or behind your back. Let's look at some of the roles the enemy plays in order to pull you away from your relationship with your Father and, thus, your calling.

1. **Deceiver**: 2 Corinthians 11:3 shows us that Satan is a deceiver. A deceiver is one who does and says anything in order to mislead. In this case, he desires to lead you away from your Father's embrace. Often he does this by corrupting the nature of that which God has created. He twists and turns things around to get his own way and to get you to believe falsehoods. Satan can mislead you into believing that your calling is entirely different from what God intended. For example, he may deceive you by telling you that you aren't really useful in God's eyes or

by causing you to be easily offended by what others say about you.

2. **Father of all lies**: Not only is Satan a deceiver, but he told the *first* lie, which began a tidal wave of lies that has been raging ever since. John 8:44 tells us that he has always hated the truth because there is no truth in him. He simply cannot tell the truth. That is because Jesus *is* the Truth. In this sense, Satan is the opposite of the Truth (but with no power). If we let him, he can fill us with his lies as well: lies like, "You're not good enough," or, "You are too ordinary to fulfill God's calling on your life." Refuse to believe those lies. Start proclaiming God's truths in every situation.

3. **Thief**: John 10:10 calls Satan a thief who comes to steal, kill, and destroy. He steals our joy, our peace, and our hope. But remember, he is the deceiver, so he often blames others for the misery he causes. Don't let him steal what God has placed in your heart. Jesus came to give us a rich and satisfying life—a life with direction and purpose. Don't let him destroy your hope in your God-given purpose.

4. **Accuser**: Have you ever found yourself caught in a web of lies? Whether you were the one telling the lies or you got caught up in someone else's lies, there is only one way to straighten everything out: to sit down with everyone present and hash out the truth. Satan is a liar, but he never wants to take credit for the chaos he creates, so he accuses the innocent. Do not let Satan's accusations about

you or your abilities stop you from what God created you for. Call out the enemy's lies for what they are: untruths about you. Tell him to be gone! You have power over him in Jesus' mighty name.

5. **Tempter**: In the book of Matthew, chapter four, we read about how Satan tempted Jesus in the wilderness. He tempted him to do and say things that were in opposition to what Jesus knew about his Father. He told Jesus, "If you are the son of God…" Satan appeared to acknowledge Jesus' birthright—that Christ was indeed the son of God—but Satan was only trying to goad him into going against the Father's will. The tempter will use anything he can to entice you into falling off the path you were designed to walk. He will tempt you away from your calling by using all sorts of schemes. He might tempt you to sin, thereby driving a wedge between you and God. Or he might tempt you to take credit for gifts related to your purpose, resulting in sinful pride that will again pull you away from an intimate relationship with your Father.

6. **Predator**: 1 Peter 5:8 shows us that the enemy prowls around like a roaring lion looking for someone to devour. Have you ever seen footage of a lioness on the hunt? They slink around in tall grass, hiding and creeping ever closer to their prey. They sneak up on their innocent victims, often getting within just a few feet without the prey even knowing it is being hunted. Then they attack with a roar. They do this in broad daylight. They go after the weak and young. You have a *real enemy* who seeks to chew you

to bits, and he will do it brazenly—out in the open. But remember, he often uses others to do his dirty work. You must recognize that when you begin pursuing your calling, the enemy will be in attack mode. Make sure you understand that attacks from others are actually attacks from Satan. He is the real enemy! The good news here is that you have a Savior whom this enemy fears. When Jesus walks in, Satan trembles. Don't forget: Greater is he that is within you!

Satan is all of the things listed above, and he is cunning. There is nothing more frightening than a psychopath with a high IQ. I am not saying this to make you feel defeated, nor to convince you that there is nothing you can do to stop his advances. The key is to go to the One who is all-knowing and all-powerful.

Satan's tricks are nothing to God. Jesus already defeated him when he went into hell and took the keys of sin and death from him. And since we are God's children, we have the same power Jesus did on that beautiful day. God's Word tells us that he will crush Satan under our feet. He has no power when we put on the whole armor of God. The first step to defeating your enemy is to read and use God's Word.

Section 2
How Do We Respond to Feelings of Being Ordinary?

When we struggle with feelings of being ordinary, we can either respond with our human nature (our flesh), or we can let God take over (the Spirit). In Section 3, we will talk about a Kingdom response, but in this section, I want to cover two human responses to "ordinary" that we might struggle with at some time in our lives and that hinder us from living lives steeped in purpose.

First, I want to make it clear that God's will for your life—whether you call it your purpose, your walk, or your calling—is multifaceted. Your Father has many things in mind for you to achieve in your lifetime. He has gifts and talents that he wants you to pursue, people he wants you to come in contact with, situations he wants you to experience, and words he wants you to hear in his time. When I use the term "purpose," I am referring to all of these things.

Four

Being Fearful of Living Out Your Calling

*P*erhaps the most common human response to God's call-ing on our lives is to run. Most of us excel at spiritual sprinting—fleeing the uncomfortable! The Bible is full of exam-ples of how God has called men and women for his purpose, many of whom chose to run in a direction that was the polar opposite of what God wanted.

The fear of living out God's calling is very common. I mean, come on! It's a terrifying thing when the Master of the Universe calls little ol' me and you to do something we feel we cannot do. Sometimes we respond like Moses or Jonah. Moses made excuses when God told him that he would be a leader of the millions of Israelites who were in captivity in Egypt. Jonah hid on a boat headed *away* from Nineveh, the city God had called on him to warn of his impending wrath. Like these two men of the Bible, we might wonder why the Lord has called us. We might say, "Go find someone more qualified," or, "I can't do it. I am not able." Perhaps we simply don't *want* to do what he asks us to do. Maybe you already know what God has called you to do, but you are not willing to do it because the risk is too great.

The issue is fear. Whether we want to acknowledge it or not, fear can stop us dead in our tracks when it comes to living out our calling. In the following pages, we will examine four areas where fear stops us from fulfilling God's purpose for our lives.

Relationships

Believe it or not, fear of living out your calling can cause you to struggle in your personal relationships. Perhaps you hide from relationships, becoming a loner or a hermit. Or you might exist on the other end of the spectrum: a people-pleaser who lets others fill a void that was created only for God to satisfy. We might fail to love as God called us to do in his Word. Often, people who are mean and rude do so out of fear that they will be hurt. They are protecting their hearts from perceived threats.

The Father created us to be in relationship with him and with others. As we have already discussed, he gave us the two greatest commandments in the New Testament: to love God and love others. He knew this would be a great challenge for us, which is why we must choose to walk in the Spirit daily in order to fulfill his will for us. Don't let fear stop you from forming and maintaining loving relationships. Healthy, godly relationships are part of God's will for your life.

Personal Image

A negative personal image is when you fail to see yourself as you really are. This could involve your outer appearance, your inner strengths, your intelligence, or your abilities. It stems from comparing yourself to others and finding yourself lacking.

God's Word says that you are fearfully and wonderfully made. A negative personal image results when you look at others, then look back at yourself and see someone who is less successful. A negative personal image could lead to psychological issues, which might manifest as bulimia, anorexia, overeating, self-mutilation, or other unhealthy habits. In fact, feeling too ordinary might lead us into dangerous situations involving physical, sexual, or emotional abuse. After all, if we believe we're nothing special, why would we think we deserve more? We are so afraid to believe what

God says about us that we will hide our overwhelming shortcomings in anything that might dull our pain.

On the other hand, the fear of being too ordinary might make us go to extremes to try to stand out. Perhaps we'll go out of our way to try to *prove* that we are not ordinary. We might dye our hair outrageous colors, wear outlandish clothing, mutilate our bodies for the sake of art, or act in some bizarre way to garner attention. To be clear, I am not saying any of these things in and of themselves is bad or against God's will. What I am saying is that the fear of being ordinary sometimes elicits strong reactions.

Women and men alike can fall victim to these fears, and sometimes it can lead us down some pretty scary paths. The issue is the motivation behind why we try to hide or stand out in a crowd. God created you the way you are, flaws and all. He loves you and calls you beautiful, handsome, talented, and loved. There is certainly nothing wrong with taking healthy pride in your appearance or your abilities, but remember to give your fears over to God and to let him speak words of peace over your situation.

For God has not given us the spirit of fear;
but of power, love, and self-discipline.

—2 Timothy 1:7 (NLT)

This verse from 2 Timothy follows a previous verse in which Paul advises Timothy to fan into flames the spiritual gift God had given him. Following our God-given purpose is not easy and often brings out great fear in us, but these feelings are not from God. God promises to give us power, love, and sound thinking.

If you are struggling with a negative personal image, claim this Word for yourself today. God has chosen you, flaws included, to satisfy his plan, and he will give you all you need to walk it out!

Professional Life

Fear of living out your calling can also affect your professional life. It can hinder you from stepping out and taking risks in the workplace. If God is in your heart, he desires to be involved in every aspect of your life, including where you spend the majority of your day. Fear of the unknown can greatly hinder any person from going above and beyond their comfort zone. Perhaps God is prompting you to apply for a promotion, and you just don't think you are qualified. Remember, if he called you to it, he will give you all you need to do it—*if* you stay rooted and grounded in him.

Maybe the Father is putting wild thoughts into your head about quitting your job and going into ministry full-time. Again, if he called you to do it, he will provide. Maybe God is prompting you to speak to a coworker or to pray about a certain need in the workplace. I know he has placed you where you are for some reason. Don't forget that a large portion of your calling involves affecting others through love. Do not let fear stop you from walking in the abundant life God has waiting for you through your career!

Spiritual Life

The last area where we often experience fear is in the spiritual realm. Fear of God's judgment and wrath can sometimes lead us to hide from what God is telling us in our hearts. This happens to many people before they come to know Christ. They hide from God, often denying he even exists. They tell themselves, "If God doesn't exist, then I am okay." Just because someone doesn't believe in God doesn't mean he doesn't exist. But even after we come to know Christ, we can still deny his truths for us. We lie to ourselves, telling ourselves that we are doing good in the areas of our lives where we struggle. We may tell ourselves that *everyone* struggles with these problems, and everyone sins. After years and years of telling ourselves that we are fine, we begin to believe our own lies—and the lies of the enemy. This path leads us to spiritual death.

Instead of being fearful of weak spiritual areas in our lives, we should surrender them to God instead. David said in Psalm 139:23–24 (NLT), "Search me, O God, and know my heart; test me and know my anxious thoughts. Point out anything in me that offends you, and lead me along the path of everlasting life."

We cannot hide from God. He sees and knows all anyway, so why not just let him help us in our weak areas? I believe that this is why God called David "a man after his own heart." David was flawed, and he knew it. He knew he was just an ordinary shepherd boy. But he also knew that God had a great plan for his life, and he always surrendered his human nature to God and let God lead him.

If you struggle in a spiritual area of your life, let go and let God take over. If you surrender it to him, he will love you back to where you need to be with a gentleness that will bring tears to your eyes and new peace to your soul.

Five

PURSUING DREAMS AND GOALS GOD NEVER GAVE US

he second possible response to feelings of being ordinary is to pursue dreams and goals that God never gave us. In order to compensate for our feelings of inadequacy, we sometimes overachieve in certain areas of our lives, or we look at what others have achieved and set our sights on *their* dreams instead of our own God-given dreams. This is a response I understand all too well.

I am a recovering people-pleaser. I am also a get-it-done workaholic. When someone even mentions that they have a problem, I want to jump in and solve it. The problem with doing this is that I don't always wait on God. He once had to tell me, "Just because you can do that doesn't mean I want you to." He has had to tell me this over and over again throughout my lifetime.

I often jump into situations with both feet. I see a need, and I want to fill it. And while this may seem harmless, the danger is that I could step outside of God's will for my life while trying to solve a problem. Can you relate? Do you find yourself exhausted and drained because you are working so hard and pouring your efforts into so many tasks that you have nothing left for yourself? Perhaps you're even working hard in a ministry or some aspect of Christian "duty" and are secretly resentful of the work. Is it possible that you are chasing a dream that God never gave you?

Again, we will look at the four areas of our lives which are affected when we pursue paths that God never gave us.

Relationships

When we pursue dreams and goals that God never gave us, it can do just as much damage to our relationships as fear. Sometimes, people who are dating are seeking a "perfect" match instead of praying for God to send them the person he has set apart for them. People often choose friends based on their own selfish desires rather than on God's will for their relationships. Not only did God have specific purposes in mind for you, but he also has specific people in mind who will encourage you and lift you up spiritually along the way. But if you are not seeking his will in every aspect of your life, you risk falling haphazardly into close relationships with anyone who happens to be around at the time.

Even though we need to be very careful about choosing the people with whom we form close alliances, we Christians do not have the luxury of having a superior attitude while living out our faith. There are no such things as elitist cliques in the Kingdom of Heaven. Our Father wishes that all would come to know him. How do others come to know him? Most often it is initially through *our* love for them. I know one thing for sure: If you cannot learn to love others, you will never get past ordinary!

God's plan for your life always includes loving others deeply as you walk down the road he planned for you. He loved you and me with an extraordinary love, and when we truly experience that love, how can we *not* love others?

Personal Image

Our feelings of being ordinary often lead us into competition with others. If we build our worth around being "better" than people around us, we may spend hours and hours focused on our looks, our job, our money, our talents, or our skills. Perhaps we begin to develop a judgmental attitude, looking down on those who cannot live up to our impossible standards. For example, women and men alike spend millions of dollars each year on elective plastic surgery in order to meet the unrealistic goal of looking perfect. Many of us look in the mirror and see "ordinary" and want so badly to rise above that. We want others to see us as beautiful or special.

God certainly gives people special gifts, talents, and abilities. I have always envied athletes; I'm so clumsy that I can barely walk in a straight line without tripping over my own two feet. I know without a shadow of a doubt that God has called some people, such as Tim Tebow, to be athletes in order to have a platform to share his goodness and love with others. There are also incredibly talented musicians who use their gifts to magnify God through praise and worship. God uses beautiful people to be models or public figures for his glory. Where we fail God is when we have the wrong motive. Remember:

> **But the Lord said to Samuel, "Don't judge by his appearance or height, for I have rejected him. The Lord doesn't see things the way you see them. People judge by outward appearance, but the Lord looks at the heart."**
>
> **—1 Samuel 16:7 (NLT)**

Accept who God created you to be. Be "okay" with that curly hair. Flaunt those freckles. Take notice of the advantages of being tall (or short, in my case). Love those curves. Have fun with your age. And, for goodness' sake, enjoy life!

Professional Life

As previously mentioned, feelings of inadequacy leave some of us with the need to overachieve. We become workaholics, pursuing fulfillment in doing a job well. We go 100 miles an hour and give 110 percent in everything we do. The problem is that we are not always pursuing dreams that God gave us. Again, this is an area where I often struggle. It led me into a career to which I was never called. It has led me into ministries for which I did not have a calling. It has led me away from what God really intended for my life.

Pride sometimes causes us to get in our own way, preventing us from doing what God desires. Sometimes we use what meager abilities we do have and get so busy doing our own thing—without God—that we soon wind up far outside of God's will. Once, while driving on the interstate, I overshot my exit by almost a hundred miles simply because I wasn't paying attention. My workaholic mind was focused on all the things I needed to get done.

Notice the prevalence of the word "I" in those last few statements. We overachievers need to realize that even though we might be hardworking people, we are still greatly flawed and *need* God's direction for our lives. We need him every moment of every day. We need to rely solely on him to lead us where *he* wants us to go.

If you are anything like me in this regard, join me today and *let go*. Rest. Be still. And let God do what he wants to do in your life and take you where he wants you to go.

Spiritual Life

In the spiritual realm, feelings of ordinary can cause us to over-compensate as well. Pursuing dreams and desires that God never gave us can leave us feeling like we have something to prove. To avoid being seen as ordinary, we seek to become super-uber-Christians. (I know this is a made-up word, but I just couldn't resist!) This uber-status can lead down two unstable paths: being legalistic and being judgmental.

Legalism is when we begin to shift our focus away from what *God* has done and onto what *we* can do. By doing so, we shift the spotlight onto ourselves. Being judgmental is no better. Since being highly spiritual requires so much work, the judgmental super-uber-Christian looks down on others who haven't yet reached that point of the journey.

I would love to tell you that I have never been guilty of making these mistakes, but the honest truth is that much of this book comes from my personal walk with God—and my own personal struggles. I have been guilty of being legalistic and of being judgmental. I have been guilty of seeking a scripture verse just so I could prove someone wrong. I have been guilty of criticizing a "baby" Christian for their struggles. And if you have been a Christian long enough, you might struggle with these issues as well.

It helps to know where these responses come from so that we can submit them to the Father. When you ask for help, he will be faithful, and he will strengthen you. He will help you love others as he loves you, if you just ask. After a particularly heart-breaking time in my life, I surrendered my misguided need to be a "spiritual giant" to God. I laid my judgmental nature at his feel (and I continue to do so every day). He has cultivated my love for others so much. I often look back and am amazed at the change in myself. And I know you will as well if you just surrender to him. Fall in love with the imperfect, perfect person God created you to be!

Section 3
Having a Kingdom Response to Feelings of Ordinary

We spent the majority of the first two sections of this book discussing the truth that we are all called according to our Father's purpose and his will for our lives, where feelings of ordinary come from, and how we often have worldly responses to these feelings of being ordinary. What does God have to say about how we should respond to his call for our lives? Can we truly live a life in which we walk according to his purpose every day? How can we have a "Kingdom response" to these desires that are buried deep within our souls? We were created to walk in this purpose every day of our lives, not just every once in a while.

> **Now all glory to God, who is able, through
> his mighty power at work within us,
> to accomplish infinitely more than we
> might ask or think. Glory to him in the**

**church and in Christ Jesus through all
generations forever and ever! Amen.**

—EPHESIANS 3:20–21 (NLT)

"Ordinary" reads the verse above and thinks, *God could do more
for me if only I asked or if only I believed more.* But what our Father
is saying here is that he is able to do infinitely more *through* us
than *to* us.

We walk around in life so unsatisfied, trying to use people or
possessions to fill a gaping hole in us. In reality, what we lack is
God working through us. Walking according to the purpose we
were called for—living out the God-given desires of our hearts—
is the most satisfying, most fulfilling, and most rewarding undertaking you will ever experience! The banquet table is set before
you. The feast is ready. Are you going to attend the party of your
life, or are you going to stay stuck in your safe little world and
miss out on what you were created to do?

Romans 12:2 (New International Version) tells us, "Do not
conform to the pattern of this world, but be transformed by the
renewing of your mind. Then you will be able to test and approve
what God's will is—his good, pleasing and perfect will."

One of the patterns of this world is to seek approval from others. We see glaring evidence of this displayed in the popularity of
social media. Just the other day, I heard two men in church having
a discussion about who had the most "likes" on Facebook. Walk
down the street and make a mental note of how many people
are on their phones. We may laugh at videos of people falling or

running into things because they are so distracted by their mobile devices, but just go to a popular sightseeing place and take notice of how many people are using their phones to take pictures of themselves with an iconic background, just so they can post it to their social media accounts.

You want to see someone smile? Just ask to take a selfie with them. All of a sudden, they are beaming as if this is the best day of their life and you're some long-lost friend. Couples who were growling at each other moments before and haven't touched all day long are suddenly hugging and grinning ear-to-ear in order to get that perfect profile picture. Meanwhile, people who try to reach out for help on social media are often seen as complaining or being negative, and they are promptly unfriended or unfollowed. What is the reason for this bizarre behavior? It's because we are so afraid someone might think less of us if they see through our fictitious, perfect lives in social media land.

We need to heed Paul's advice in Romans 12.

> **Don't copy the behavior and customs of this world, but let God transform you into a new person by changing the way you think. Then you will learn to know God's will for you, which is good and pleasing and perfect.**
>
> **—Romans 12:2 (NLT)**

If we look like the world, sound like the world, dress like the world, talk like the world, and act like the world, how are we being transformed? Here, God's words tell us that transformation will bring about a change in the way we think. But before we can be transformed, we are advised not to conform to the world's standards. To "conform," in this context, means to seek to mimic others—to look and act just like everyone else. We do this because we think they will somehow love us more if we are more like them.

As I have previously mentioned, the reason I'm so familiar with the issue of people-pleasing is because I have so often struggled with this issue myself. It is an innate struggle with pleasing people that I will never completely be able to overcome. It is a "thorn to my flesh," as the Apostle Paul mentioned. My "flesh" wants to please people, and when I become too tightly focused on pleasing others, I lose focus on what God has called me to do.

My dear friend, you were created uniquely for God's purpose in your life. There is no one and has never been anyone just like you on earth. Don't lose sight of God's perfect will for your life because you're distracted by everyone's perfect—and perfectly fake—lives as portrayed on the Internet!

For me, the transformation of my mind when I began this book was for me to get off of social media. I don't mean I canceled all of my accounts; I just don't check my phone every ten minutes to see who "liked" my post or to check on what's going on with everyone else. I cannot tell you how freeing this was for me. I did not even realize the extent to which social media was causing my anxiety level to increase until I went a week without constantly logging in. Suddenly, I had more time, and my mind was freer to listen to the Father's whispers throughout the day.

There are many distractions that can lead you away from your calling. Maybe, unlike me, you don't have an issue with social media. What do *you* need to do in order to not be conformed to this world? What do you need to cut out of your everyday life or start doing so that you can walk down the path you have dreamed of for so long? How can you shift your focus off of the things in the world and back onto your heavenly Father and his plan for your life?

One of my favorite scriptures in the Bible is Isaiah 26:3 (NLT): "You will keep in perfect peace all who trust in you, all whose thoughts are fixed on you!" This verse has always spoken volumes to me because no matter what I am going through, if I can just get my mind on God, he brings sweet, perfect peace to my soul. Getting our minds on him means knowing him and spending time with him every day. It means having him as the center of our focus. It means that there is two-way communication. In order to know and walk according to your God-given calling, there are some very important steps that each one of us must work through, and I want to share those with you in the following chapters.

Six

What is Your Unique Purpose?

$\mathcal{T}$he first stage of stepping into your God-given calling is to know exactly what your Father God has called you to do. As I mentioned before, God has many things he wants you to accomplish in your lifetime. God has tiny little details that he wants us to attend to each and every day: loving the unlovable, showing grace and kindness to strangers as well as friends and family, praying for others, and meeting the needs of people around us. The list is endless.

Our calling is not necessarily a destination but a journey where we walk through situations and come into contact with people God wants us to impact. God's Word is full of guidance for that journey. It guides us to live a lifestyle steeped in love and forgiveness. We are the walking, talking body of Christ.

But here's the deal: I cannot reach everyone with the Gospel. Billy Graham couldn't reach everyone. Missionaries cannot reach everyone. Your pastor/minister/priest cannot reach everyone. We—the body of Christ—have to work together to cover the earth with the good news that Jesus loves everyone and came to die for their sins. We must show them, in our own special way, how he loves them. This is why God needs you. He needs your abilities, talents, insights, brokenness, struggles, and influence to reach a lost and dying world. There is no one on this earth like you. No person has the same physical makeup as you. No other person has been through the same experiences as you or possesses the thoughts you do.

With that being said, what we can do is explore *how* God wishes you to share the Gospel. Remember what I mentioned in the introduction to this book—about how you might have secret yearnings deep within you, the desires of your heart? This is a wonderful place to start when discovering how to fulfill what God has called you to do in this life. I would like to take you on an exploratory journey to help you find some of the paths God is leading you down.

Brainstorm for a few minutes and name five desires of your heart. Dig deep, my friend. No one is going to read this unless you show them, so be honest. Take some time. Pray that God would remind you of these deepest desires. What do you dream about when your mind is most at rest? What did you dream about doing as a child but put away when you grew up? Some of these dreams/desires may be quite obvious to you. You might already be pursuing some of them. Other desires might seem frivolous or silly. Some might seem incredibly small or insignificant. I don't want you to analyze them. Just write them down. If you have more than five, write them down as well. But let's get started with at least five.

_____

_____

_____

_____

_____

Now, I want you to find and research at least three verses of scripture that mention some aspect of each of the desires you just wrote down. Make a note of the three verses on the lines above after each desire. For example, for my desire to be a writer, I found a scripture in Proverbs 7:3 about writing God's instructions deep within my heart. In fact, I found many verses about writing God's commands and lessons on my heart. I found this very enlightening because, as I currently write this, God is taking something that was previously only a dream and making it a reality. I believe He will do this for you as well.

Let me tell you, there is *nothing more momentous* in your life than when you hear God speaking to you directly about what he has called you to do. I can still remember the day I was sitting in church as my pastor spoke about fulfilling a calling. God spoke directly to me through the Scriptures read by the pastor. I thought my heart was going to beat out of my chest as I suddenly realized that God *wanted* me to pursue my dream of writing.

I couldn't breathe. I felt as though the world had stopped for a moment. I knew I had always had the desire to write, but the idea that God was the source of that desire—and that he truly wanted me to pursue it—ignited a flame in my being and set a fire deep in my soul. But as thrilling as that was, I could have easily hidden that moment in my heart and let that fire die down and fade away. I could have kept this revelation to myself. If I had, you and I both know what I would have done. I would have told myself that it really wasn't that important, or I would have listened to what others—or Satan—had to say about the matter. Within a week, I might have effectively convinced myself that writing could wait until a better time, or that I simply couldn't do it and was too ordinary to accomplish such a feat.

Let us now go beyond writing down and researching scripture verses that pertain to your calling. I ask you, dear friend, to go a step further.

As our ancestors did, let us make a momentous occasion out of this revelation from God, which is exactly what this is. A revelation is when our eyes are opened to truths that already exist. It is nothing new. God thought about your purpose long before he created you. He included it in your DNA while you were being formed in your mother's womb. Your purpose is already inside you. You just might not understand it yet. Like John the Revelator and Paul the Apostle, let us document this revealing of truth from the Father.

We are beginning to see the true purpose for which we were created. Abraham, Moses, and many of our forefathers built altars to commemorate momentous occasions. As God reveals his calling to you, take time to stop, thank him for what he has done and is going to do in and through you, and ask for his guidance for the future. I'm not sure how you picture the ultimate realization of your God-given purpose, but I recommend that you take time to acknowledge what God is saying to your heart.

I do not believe that every desire you wrote has to be pursued at this very moment. Each of those desires was crafted by God for a specific time, purpose, and season.

For everything there is a season, a time for every activity under heaven. A time to be born and a time to die. A time to plant and a time to harvest. A time to kill and a time to heal. A time to tear down and a time to build up. A time to cry and a time to laugh. A time to grieve and a time to dance. A time to scatter stones and a time to gather stones.

**A time to embrace and a time to turn away. A
time to search and a time to quit searching.
A time to keep and a time to throw away.
A time to tear and a time to mend. A time
to be quiet and a time to speak. A time to
love and a time to hate. A time for war and a
time for peace. What do people really get for
all their hard work? I have seen the burden
God has placed on us all. Yet God has made
everything beautiful for its own time. He
has planted eternity in the human heart, but
even so, people cannot see the whole scope
of God's work from beginning to end.**

—ECCLESIASTES 3:1–11 (NLT)

Pray over those desires and God's timing. Ask your Father which
desires he wants you to pursue at this time. I do believe that he is
asking you to pursue at least one of those desires. Otherwise, he
would not have brought them to your mind.

Copy down what you wrote in the blanks above on a note-
card and put it in your wallet. Write them on your bathroom
mirror. Print them out and hang them in your closet. Write them
in a journal. Just put them in a place where you will see them
more than once a day. Pray over them every time you see the
list. I promise, you will be amazed by how God opens your eyes
and reveals opportunities to fulfill your calling if only you give
him a chance. And the list you created might be changed as God

continues to reveal his nature to you. Your eyes will begin to be opened to what God already knows about you.

Just this morning, as I was lying in bed (not quite ready to get up and tackle my busy day), God revealed that the true calling behind my desire to write was a deeper calling to love others. Writing is merely my opportunity to love and serve others. Hopefully, I can help people grow closer to God. What better way to love people than to lead them to my Father or to help them strengthen their relationship with him?

Lastly, you need to *tell someone* about any desire that you know God is asking you to pursue. Share it with a close friend, a family member, or perhaps your pastor or youth minister—one person you can trust. Tell someone who will take this seriously and will encourage you to pursue your God-given calling in a godly manner.

Don't just share a tiny piece of your dream in casual conversation. Make it a point to have an in-depth conversation. Call them up and ask if they have a couple of hours to speak with you. Share everything God is telling you. Ask them to pray with you, ask them for advice, and ask them to help hold you accountable. Don't let yourself off the hook by letting the dream die. The more trusted people you tell, the more you will commit yourself to fulfilling your calling.

Seven

GO!

Now that you have explored the desires God has placed on your heart, *get busy*! Go!

When we read about the apostles in the New Testament, we discover a common theme. When the apostles first encountered Jesus and were asked to follow him, they often dropped what they were doing and followed him immediately. They got up, and they went. Similarly, Abraham's calling in the Old Testament took him away from his family and even his country, and Paul's calling on the road to Damascus brought blindness.

Okay, so I understand that these might seem a little drastic, but the point I am trying to make here is that none of these people stopped to wonder if they were qualified. Because the reality is, they weren't. All they knew was that God had called them to go, so they went.

Ordinary says you need to wait until you are trained or gain the right skills or education. *Ordinary* says that your calling rests somewhere in the future. But God has already placed his desires in your heart, and his Word says that he will go before you and equip you to fulfill his calling. If he says "go," respond. Start today.

If you're anything like me, you currently have no clue how to begin to fulfill your calling. When I shared with my husband that I felt God had called me to write and that I truly wanted to realize this calling, I also shared my doubts about my ability. I told him I just didn't think I could do it but that I was relying on God to help me. He stared at me as if I was a complete moron. Then he said, "Candy, you just completed your master's degree. What have you been complaining about for the last five years? Writing!" He was right. Over the course of those five years, I had probably written four or five books' worth of essays and research papers. (That's what getting a master's degree is all about: reading, doing research, and writing papers.)

Perhaps God has given you a desire that you feel totally unprepared for. I promise that if it is a calling that God intends for you to pursue today, he has already been preparing you for it in some way! Don't worry about whether or not you can do it. Just be obedient and go. Get started today.

Once again, please let me assist you, dear friend, in discovering what God might be saying to your heart. Revisit the five dreams or desires you wrote down. I asked you to pray over which one God is asking you to pursue immediately. I hope you have done that already. If not, please do so now.

Just as there is nothing more satisfying than walking according to the plan God has for you, there is nothing more *frustrating* than trying to walk according to a plan God did not intend for you to step into at this time in your life! But if God gives you the green light, get started in some small way—today. Think of a small action you can take to begin your journey.

In the third chapter of Joshua, we find that as the children of Israel were traveling through the wilderness and reached the Jordan River (which was flooding at the time), God had a plan about how to get all those people across the river. God told Joshua to have the priests carry the Ark of the Covenant to the water's edge and to step into the water. As soon as the priest's feet touched the edge of the water, the water above that point began to back up, and the water below flowed away, so that the people walked across the river on dry land. Notice that it says nowhere in this scripture that God told Joshua or any of the children of Israel what was going to happen. He told them what to do, and they simply did it. I bet those priests thought they would be swept away by the raging river, but nonetheless, they were obedient.

If God has called you to do something, you need to take the first step. What can you do today to begin your journey? If he has asked you to preach, perhaps you need to sit down with the Word and begin composing a sermon (even if you have no one to preach it to!). If you long to sing or make music, buy an instrument or sign up for the church choir. If you want to help others, begin researching the needs in your community or those at large. I don't know what God is whispering to your heart, but remember that his words do not stop; they vibrate into eternity. Get up and get moving to the rhythm of his voice!

But here is the most important advice I can give you: Once you get up and begin moving, don't stop. You will be wobbly at first—like a young infant who begins to toddle with his first steps. Your strength will grow as the Father fills you with his strength and purpose. Remember: If God is for you, then who/what can stand against you?

Eight

Knowing Your Creator

$\mathcal{I}$n order to live out the calling for which you were created, *you must intimately know your Creator*. And to know your Creator, you must know his Word. This is one of the few times in this book where I will use the word "must." I feel that strongly about it.

You see, apart from your Creator, you do not exist. He is not like a piece of clothing that you put on, dressing up only on Sundays. He isn't a genie in a bottle whose purpose is granting your every wish. Without him, there would be no "us." And the only way to truly know him is to visit the only physical revelation he left of himself on this earth: The Bible. If we are designed to accomplish his plans, where else should we go to find the blueprint than from the Master Architect?

Let me explain. Scientists have known for many centuries that we inherit our traits from our parents. In the last seventy-five years, scientists have gained further understanding of how genes pass on the traits of living things. From the 1990s through the early part of the twenty-first century, researchers began to map out the human genome, and geneticists are now using that information to further research on treating illnesses through gene therapy. We are truly just beginning to understand the human blueprint: the instructions for our bodies. I expect that with the discovery of the full set of instructions for our bodies will come many breakthroughs in understanding and treating disease processes. In the past, medicine focused solely on treating the symptoms of genetic diseases and cancers, never fully comprehending how to "fix" the problems. Without intimate knowledge of the "plans," efforts didn't always bring about results. In the same way, we need intimate knowledge of the plans—and the plan-maker—before we can live in wholeness and spiritual health.

Reading the Bible isn't like reading an owner's manual, however. We cannot read it once and fully comprehend all that it has to say. Don't forget that God's Word is dynamic. It is living. Its meaning for us can change based on what God is trying to speak into our lives. The Bible is God's revelation to man, and it cannot be fully comprehended in one reading. The Writer will only open our eyes to what he wants to speak to us at any given time because we are mere mortals and incapable of understanding all of his truths at once.

> **"Look, God is greater than
> we can understand."**
>
> **—Job 36:26 (NLT)**

"My thoughts are nothing like your
thoughts," says the Lord. "And my ways are
far beyond anything you could imagine. For
just as the heavens are higher than the earth,
so my ways are higher than your ways and
my thoughts higher than your thoughts."

—Isaiah 55:8–9 (NLT)

Now our knowledge is partial and
incomplete, and even the gift of prophecy
reveals only part of the whole picture! But
when full understanding comes, these
partial things will become useless.

—1 Corinthians 13:9–10 (NLT)

The understanding of our Creator occurs over time, with God revealing his ways to us through tiny glimpses here and there. Our human minds cannot understand him fully, but we can grow in our knowledge through revelations found in the Scriptures.

For most of my younger years, I read the Bible, although I didn't read it every day. Often when I would read, I would do it marathon style—trying to get in a much as possible but not fully comprehending everything I read. At one point, I decided that I really did need to read it daily, so I purchased a Bibles designed to be read through in its entirety within one year. It was a good idea, but to me, it became a mindless chore.

As I grew in my faith, I began to desire more from God's Word, and so I changed my approach to how I read his Word. I now read to learn more about my Father. I long to *know* him, so I try to focus on quality, not quantity, in reading his Word. I don't know what works for you, but you need to be reading God's Word in order to learn more about your Father and to develop a more intimate relationship with him. Perhaps a strict daily routine works for you. Maybe you would prefer journaling Bibles or the Bibles with space to draw or take notes in the margins. Listening to the Bible in audio format can also be very enlightening if you are an auditory learner. Whatever works best for you is what you should do.

The key takeaway here is that in order for you to fulfill your calling, you must understand your Father as deeply as your human mind will allow. Whether you are reading or listening to the Word, God promises that his Holy Spirit will enable you to understand his ways.

For, "Who can know the Lord's thoughts? Who knows enough to teach him?" But we understand these things, for we have the mind of Christ.

—1 Corinthians 2:16 (NLT)

"But when the Father sends the Advocate as my representative—that is, the Holy

**Spirit—he will teach you everything and will
remind you of everything I have told you."**

—John 14:26 (NLT)

I think we ordinary people often become intimidated when it comes to "studying" God's Word. Even as I was researching the scriptures above, I began telling myself that I was merely explaining what people already know. Dark thoughts flooded my mind about how unqualified I was to teach this topic. But God's Word is the great equalizer. The same innate amount of God's power exists in his Word when I speak it as when any great theologian speaks it. I don't care if you possess the greatest possible ability to understand the written or spoken Word or if you are struggling to learn the basics; God's Word is God's Word, and his Word will *never* be void. It can *never* be canceled, made invalid, or found empty!

If you read just one verse a day, I promise that God will use that single verse to reveal himself to you just as effectively as if you were to read twenty verses. But if God has impressed upon you to read more than one verse a day, then you must be diligent to fulfill his wishes .

There is one last issue that we need to address, and that is the subject of Bible studies. Bible studies written by Christian authors encouraging you to be in the Word are certainly beneficial for helping you learn more about the Father and his plan for you. I have a few favorites, but the key is to find an author who speaks your language—someone who writes in a style you can easily understand. Most importantly, make sure that if you choose a Bible Study, it points you to many verses of scriptures and that the teaching lines up with God's Word. Do some research. Find out what respectable people in the publishing business are saying about these authors. Ask your pastor to recommend some writers.

But here's the catch when it comes to using Bible studies: They can never replace the time you spend in the Word. Use them as jumping-off points. Let them instruct you. Allow them to get you thinking about God's Word and ignite a fire in you. But never let a human author become the focus of that fire; they should point you to the true Light.

Daily devotions are another great source to remind us of God's Word. I receive a scripture each day through several media sources, and they often appear right when I need to hear God's voice. God's Word is often called the "Bread of Life," giving us life-sustaining nourishment from our Great Provider. Daily devotions are like snacks throughout the day. They provide that little pick-me-up that you might need in the middle of a busy day, but, on their own, they are not enough to sustain you for a long period of time. You need the Bread of Life if you are ever to move beyond ordinary and step into the extraordinary!

Nine

Talking with Your Father

Another avenue for spending time with your Father and getting to know him better is to make time in your day for prayer. This is an integral part of your daily walk with God if you wish to experience his will and purpose for your life. Prayer is essential.

**The Lord is close to all who call on him,
yes, to all who call on him in truth.**

—Psalm 145:18 (NLT)

**One day Jesus told his disciples
a story to show that they should
always pray and never give up.**

—Luke 18:1 (NLT)

I know people who pray the most elegant prayers. I love to listen to them pray—they phrase their petitions to God so eloquently! In the past, I was very intimidated by these people. I have done my best to craft masterful prayers like theirs, but in the end, such prayers just feel empty because I wasn't being truly honest with God. I wasn't being authentic with God, and I wasn't being true to who I really was. Remember, I'm an "ordinary" woman. I speak very plainly, and I am often blunt. One day, to my surprise, a lady in my church told me that she *loved* listening to me pray because my prayers were so simple but so heartfelt. She said that she envied the way I prayed to God like he was standing next to me.

His Word tells us that he is close to *all* who call on him. This means that he listens just as closely to my ordinary prayers as he did to great clerics like John Wesley, Charles Spurgeon, or Martin Luther. Max Lucado has nothing on me. It's like having the president's personal cell phone number and the ability to call him with any issue or just to chat. Maybe that analogy falls a bit short, but the fact of the matter is that anytime I want to, I can chat with the Creator of the universe, and he is all ears. He listens intently.

Don't worry about anything; instead, pray about everything. Tell God what you need and thank him for all he has done. Then you will experience God's peace, which exceeds anything we can understand. His peace will guard your hearts and minds as you live in Christ Jesus.

—PHILIPPIANS 4:6–7 (NLT)

The *guarding* here refers to his Spirit protecting our minds from thoughts of "less than." When we pray and then thank God for what he has done in our lives (you can start by thanking him for salvation), his Spirit brings peace—peace that surpasses all understanding. Peace that will allow the arrows others hurl at you to bounce right off. Peace that will allow you to accept what the Father has created you to be. Peace that will let you see once and for all that you are not ordinary. You are extraordinary, and you were created to dance like no one is watching.

Perhaps where we (you and me, emphasis on me) need a little work in our conversations with our Father is the *listening* part. Have you ever had a conversation with someone who never lets you get a word in? They dominate the conversation and often interrupt you. And when they do stop talking long enough to give you a chance to speak, they're just thinking of what they will say next. Guilty! I am a very verbose person, in case you cannot tell. I love to express my ideas. Where I struggle, and you might too, is in truly listening.

Perhaps you have never heard the audible voice of God. His Word tells us that he often speaks to us in a still, small voice. That means we must stop moving, be still, and be quiet in order to hear what he is saying. He can speak to us in many ways: through that still small voice in our head, through his Word when we read it, through a pastor's sermon, through a song, or through the words of a friend. Our job here is to be a great listener.

If we study the Lord's prayer in the Gospels, we find that Jesus gave us a pattern for prayers.

"Our Father which art in heaven, Hallowed
by thy name. Thy Kingdom come. Thy will

**be done in earth, as it is in heaven. Give
us this day our daily bread. And forgive us
our debts, as we forgive our debtors. And
lead us not into temptation, but deliver us
from evil: For thine is the kingdom, and
the power, and the glory, forever. Amen."**

—MATTHEW 6:9–13 (KING JAMES VERSION)

Jesus started out his well-known prayer by acknowledging who God was, then praising him. He then went on to ask that God's will would be carried out on the earth (his Kingdom come). He asked for provision, forgiveness of sins, and God's strength to overcome Satan's attacks.

I think that we often read or say this prayer without ever thinking about that middle part that speaks to God's will. Remember: God's will is often carried out by his people. So if Jesus felt that this was so crucial—crucial enough to mention in a prayer that he provided as a pattern for all believers to follow—don't you think we should give the idea of praying for God's will a little more attention?

Being in prayer and listening for God's voice is especially critical when we are seeking to walk according to our calling. "May your will be done on earth" must have been one of the hardest things Jesus ever requested of his Father. He knew what that would mean for him. It meant the cross and the pain and suffering that came with it. Yet he still prayed for it and for the strength to live out his Father's will. It was God's will for Jesus to endure the cross, and Jesus obeyed.

I am not saying that God's will is for us to also endure a cross; that is an undertaking we were never asked to carry out. We are not capable of doing what Jesus did. We do, however, have a purpose for which we were specifically created, and praying for that purpose to be carried out in us each time we pray is just as important to us as it was to Jesus.

> **And this is the confidence that we have toward him, that if we ask anything according to his will he hears us.**
>
> **—1 John 5:14 (English Standard Version)**

Notice that this verse states that if we ask according to His will, he will hear us. Have you ever asked God for something and not received it? Perhaps it was for something you really wanted or something you desperately needed. And yet it didn't happen. What does this mean?

God's ways are not our ways, and his thoughts are not our thoughts. He sees the big picture. He sees everyone involved. He knows all the situations. He knows the plan he has for every person involved, and he knows what he is trying to accomplish for each of them. God is beyond three-dimensional; he is omnidimensional. We cannot even begin to understand what he is doing. All *we* see is what he places in front of us today, and that truly is all that we humans can handle. It causes us to place our trust in him each day, seeking his will as a blindfolded person trusts others for guidance.

If you know that God has placed a desire in your heart and you are seeking his guidance on how to follow that desire as he intended, he will give you guidance. I once prayed for five years for God to provide my family with a home to purchase. It was a desire I had deep in my heart. We had worked at a Christian retreat ranch for a couple of years and then moved several times. I longed for my own home, but no matter how hard we worked, no matter what we tried, the door never opened.

I was praying about this one night and asked God why he wouldn't answer my prayer. I *deserved* a home—my family deserved a home to call their own. Why wouldn't he give this to us? Do you know what he said to me? He told me to stop asking. I kid you not. In fact, I was praying and writing in a journal, and when I stopped writing, I realized that at the bottom of the page I was on, there was a quote that said to "stop asking in vain." When I read it, I knew that God was speaking to me about the house.

Talk about seeing the writing on the wall! I got the message, but I still didn't understand. Why would God tell me to stop asking for something as essential as a home? Still, I decided to heed his request and stopped praying about it.

Within a few months, my husband was offered a wonderful job in another city, and we ended up moving. It occurred to me that if we had purchased a home in the city where I had been praying to find one, we probably would not have moved, and I am quite certain that I would not be writing this book right now.

Seeking God's will for your life is infinitely more important than any of your temporary desires. Remember, he is a good Father and desires what is best for his children!

Ten

Don't Walk the Path Alone

One of the keys to unlocking opportunities and building the strength to live out your passion is to choose godly, motivated, and lovingly supportive people to walk the path with you. As I mentioned earlier, people either lift you up or drag you down. When you set out to walk according to the calling God has on your life, the people you surround yourself with and the people you form alliances with are fundamental to whether or not you stay true to the course. I am quite sure that no one ever *intentionally* forms a bond with someone who hinders them. In reality, you sort of stumble into relationships with people, and then, before you know it, you have developed strong ties with them.

Remember that you were created by the Father for a purpose, and he calls you chosen, set apart, and a child of the King. 2 Corinthians 6:14 (King James Version) tells us that we should not be "unequally yoked" with unbelievers. The NLT words the same scripture this way: "Don't team up with those who are unbelievers."

As Christians, we need to reach out to the unbeliever. It is our number-one job! But when it comes to forming close relationships, we should seek out believers, and if we want to take that a step further, we should reach out to those who have similar callings or those who support our calling. These people are found in the body of Christ.

> **Let us hold tightly without wavering to the hope we affirm, for God can be trusted to keep his promise. Let us think of ways to motivate one another to acts of love and good works. And let us not neglect our meeting together, as some people do, but encourage one another, especially now that the day of his return is drawing near.**

> **—HEBREWS 10:25 (NLT)**

Walking this path will not be easy. There will be distractions. Satan will try to discourage you and trip you up any way he can. You will find yourself falling back into the state of "ordinary," but a sure-fire way to combat all of these attacks is to find people who are moving in the same direction as you. Like-minded people will inspire you to persevere. I am willing to bet that you have experienced this phenomenon in your life. Perhaps you have coworkers who push you to be a better employee. Maybe your spouse encourages you to be a more loving partner. Or maybe you have experienced the polar opposite: people who pull you down and discourage you with their negativity.

> **"As iron sharpens iron, so a
> friend sharpens a friend."**
>
> **—Proverbs 27:17 (NLT)**

In my life, I have had the great privilege of having godly friends who have helped mold me into the woman of God I am today. These people indeed sharpened me. Sometimes they encouraged me. Other times they corrected me. Having trusted friends who gently shift my direction back to God at all times is an enormous blessing, and it is something you should pray for. I cannot say that I have had a great number of these types of close friends, but I believe quality is the key here, not quantity.

Being a part of the body of Christ also means that you actively participate in and contribute to a local body of Christ: the church. You must find a church that welcomes you and your calling, digs deep into God's Word, and loves the community around you. Being a part of a local body is a wonderful opportunity for you to explore your calling. Whatever desire God has placed in your heart, he has done so to benefit others. What better way to show God's love than to support a church that meets the needs of your community?

If you are not already committed to a local body, please pray long and hard about where God wants you to be. Praying about where you should be attending church is central to fulfilling the God-given calling for your life. Choose a church body where you can pursue your passion or one that supports you as you venture out into the community or the world.

When you seek to pursue your dreams and your purpose in a church body, ordinary is sure to rear its ugly head. It will be tempting to compare yourself to others who are pursuing similar passions. For many years, I struggled in a private hell in my own mind almost every Sunday where I would critique everything I was doing, all while comparing myself to others. I would pray and pray, submitting my thoughts to God, yet still find no peace. I was too busy looking at others and then looking at myself—and finding myself lacking. In fact, I was so busy doing this that I missed out on what God was trying to show me.

God has called you for a specific purpose. No one else has the unique calling on their life that you do. Stop trying to be like others. You only need to be the best you that God has called you to be!

Friend, please do not get so caught up in what others are doing them that you miss what God is whispering to your heart. There may be other pastors, other singers, other musicians, other speakers, other teachers, other outreach people, other prayer warriors, other dancers, or other writers in your church, but none of them are *you*! Be okay with who God created you to be. Rest in the sweet knowledge that no one can be like you.

Eleven

Show Your Father Some Love

What comes to mind when someone says "worship"? Do you think of the part of a church service where people sing hymns or praise songs? Worship is so much more than that. Worship is showing and telling God how awesome he is. Sure, you can do this with a song, but you can do it in many other ways as well.

How do you express to God just how wonderful he is to you? Worship can be a part of prayer in which you simply tell God how much you love him and how appreciative you are for all that he has done for you. It could be living your life in a way that honors him. It could mean paying your tithe of 10 percent or more to the body of Christ. It could be spending private time with him in meditation. Worship could also be a part of your testimony—what you tell others about the greatness of the God you serve. Worship is essential, and it takes on thousands of forms. You see, worship is not really an act; it is an attitude. It is a must when living out your calling.

When you put God first in your life, you are worshipping him. The first commandment in the Old Testament is to have no other gods before the One True God. The greatest commandment in the New Testament is to love God with your whole soul, strength, and mind. I think it is clear that God desires for us to worship him.

> **But the time is coming—indeed it's here now—when true worshipers will worship the Father in spirit and in truth. The Father is looking for those who will worship him that way. For God is Spirit, so those who worship him must worship in spirit and in truth.**
>
> **—JOHN 4:23–24 (NLT)**

In this verse, Jesus was speaking to the Samaritan woman at the well when he made this statement. The issue arose regarding the best place to worship. Notice that Jesus did not say that the best place of worship was a church. No, he spoke about an attitude. He said that true worship was done in Spirit and in truth. Remember that the Spirit is what is opposite of the flesh. And truth is only found in Jesus—the Way, the Truth, and the Life (John 14:6).

> **And so, dear brothers and sisters, I plead with you to give your bodies to God because of**

**all he has done for you. Let them be a living
sacrifice – the kind he will find acceptable.
This is truly the way to worship him. Don't
copy the behavior and customs of this
world, but let God transform you into a new
person by changing the way you think. Then
you will learn to know God's will for you,
which is good and pleasing and perfect.**

—ROMANS 12:1–2 (NLT)

Let's dissect the scripture above. The second part of this verse about transformation was cited earlier in this book, but now, let's add the first verse. In order to learn God's will for you and to carry it out in a good, pleasing, and perfect way, we must submit our bodies—mind, spirit, and heart—to God as a sacrifice and this is the way to truly worship him. The Apostle Paul went on to say that we do this by not copying the behaviors and customs of this world but by letting God change the way we think.

Is your worship transforming the way you think? Has the way God transformed your mind changed the way you worship? You cannot have an intimate relationship with the Father without him changing you, and that change should bring about worship through the demonstration of how much we love him.

At the time of this writing, my husband and I have been married for over twenty-five years. We had been dating for a few months when he told me he loved me, and a few months after that, he proposed. We were married when we told each other "I do" those many years ago, promising that we would always love each other. But we didn't stop saying "I love you" after we said "I do."

As for God, he loves you with a love that goes beyond earthly love between people. He loves you so much because he created you. He needed you. He wanted you. He called you to a purpose in his Kingdom. When you said "I do" to Christ, you entered into an intimate relationship with him. Have you told him lately that you love him? Have you shown him just how much?

Twelve

STAY HUMBLE

The last step to having a Kingdom response to feelings of "ordinary" is to stay humble.

The truth is, you probably really are just an ordinary person like me—in the world's eyes. But in God's eyes, you were designed for a purpose, and so you are extraordinary! Realize that you cannot fill that empty void that comes with the knowledge of being ordinary until you walk according to the calling God has for your life. Also realize that you cannot do it on your own. But the awesome thing is that you *don't have* to do it on your own. Your Father's wisdom, strength, and love are all available for the asking.

What does it mean to be humble? Let's look at several aspects of humility.

God opposes the proud but favors the humble. So humble yourselves before God. Resist the devil, and he will flee from you. Come close to God, and God will come close to you. Wash your hands, you sinners; purify your hearts, for your loyalty is divided between God and the world… Humble yourselves before the Lord, and he will lift you up in honor.

—JAMES 4:6–10 (NLT)

The Greek word for humble in the above scripture is *tapeinóō*. Strong's Concordance indicates that this type of humility "happens by being fully dependent on the Lord—dismissing reliance upon *self* (*self*-government) and *emptying carnal ego*. This *exalts the Lord* as our all-in-all and prompts the gift of his fullness in us." Being humble before God means lowering yourself in his presence.

The image I received when I read this scripture was of a peasant kneeling before his powerful king. The next time you start to feel "too ordinary" to fulfill God's calling for your life, recognize that you do need God's help. Without him, you will be just another ordinary person. But when you begin to realize what he has designed you to do—and when you begin to operate in his power and strength—overwhelming delight will come into your life. There is nothing more fulfilling or more satisfying than to do what you were created to do! We must also stay humble before others.

**Do nothing out of selfish ambition
or vain conceit. Rather, in humility
value others above yourselves.**

—PHILIPPIANS 2:3 (NIV)

**Pride ends in humiliation, while
humility brings honor.**

—PROVERBS 29:23 (NLT)

As we saw earlier, sometimes feeling ordinary can bring out a response in us, and sometimes that response is to shut out those feelings and replace them with self-pride. We begin to lift ourselves up into a position where we are above others in an effort to tamp down those feelings of inadequacy. God knows this about us and asks us to remain humble. Having a Kingdom response to those feelings simply means admitting that we are broken and that we need him. This allows us to remove harmful pride from our lives and empowers us to value others. We then are able to come full circle, back to the greatest commandment: loving God and loving others.

Humbling yourself also allows God the freedom to work out your calling. When you are humble, it means you are submissive to your Father, waiting patiently for his direction in your life. This brings us to what I believe is the greatest key to living out our purpose. Being obedient and surrendering your life to the Father is the most significant act that you can do to further your walk with God.

**So humble yourselves under the
mighty power of God, and at the right
time he will lift you up in honor**

—1 Peter 5:6 (NLT)

Humbling yourself under the mighty power of God is like the scenario I described previously; we are loyal subjects to the King. If we aren't willing to submit to his authority, we will never be able to live out our calling, no matter how hard we try.

I know that having a subservient heart is difficult. After all, it's your life, right? You should be able to live it as you want. Well, you can try that for a while, but you will eventually come to the realization that you are nothing without him.

Our way leads to brokenness and heartache. God's way leads to life—and a more abundant life.

Epilogue: Our Journey Has Just Begun!

For many years, a handwritten sign hung on my refrigerator that read, "I don't want to merely exist. I want to live in the fullness of what God has in store for me today." We moved several times, and that sign was put back on the fridge each time. People would walk into my home and give me strange looks after seeing my crumpled, food-stained reminder. I think my family probably wanted to throw it away after a while, but I kept it there because I needed to remind myself of my heart's longing.

Being an adult, a parent, an employee, a spouse, a friend, a church volunteer, and someone who is tasked with fulfilling all of our other "duties" of life can distract us from the desires God placed in our hearts long ago. It is easy to lose the wonder and curiosity we had as children. We get so stuck in providing a home and making an income that we forget what we were actually created to do.

You see, my dear friend, I want to live that *abundant life* God's Word speaks about. For too many years, I lived feeling as if the state of "ordinary" was going to consume me. My heart ached, and my soul yearned for more. Yet I knew that God was taking me on a journey. I knew that he was developing something in me. And I knew that whatever it was, I was supposed to share it with others.

I am so glad we have taken this journey out of hopelessly *ordinary* together, and I am eager to see where God is going to take us both! I ask that you please think long and hard about all that you have read in this book. Pray about what you know God is calling you to do. Seek him. Seek the desires that he placed in your heart.

You are not hopeless, and you are not ordinary. You were created according to the Master's plan, and he calls you extraordinary!

References

Definition of Desire. (n.d.). Retrieved April 17, 2019, from https://www.merriam-webster.com/dictionary/desire

Delighting in the Lord. (n.d.). Retrieved April 17, 2019, from https://hebrew4christians.com/Meditations/Desires/desires.html

Whether You Believe You Can Do a Thing or Not, You Are Right. February 3 2015, from https://quoteinvestigator.com/2015/02/03/you-can/

5013. tapeinoó. (n.d.). Retrieved April 17, 2019, from https://biblehub.com/greek/5013.htm

9 781093 166064